AF488928
Author: Ali S. Mughal

Hi friends, I am Ali,
and this is my Best friend, Mr. Car!

Let us learn with me what makes the car go vroooommmmmmm!!!

The Engine
The engine is like the heart of the car, keeps everything going!

Can you guess where the engine is in your car?

Wheels
Wheels are like the shoes of the car.
They help the car Rollllllllllll!!!

STOP
CROSS
Can you guess which part helps me stop at the traffic signal?

The
Brakes!!!

Now let's talk about my favorite Part.
The Steering Wheel!

weeeeeeeeeeeeeee!!!
The steering wheel helps my car turn.

Did you know about this pipe that makes clouds in the back?

This is where the car breathes out after all that hard work of driving you around.

GAS STATION
GAS
GAS
Can you guess
which part is
coming next?

FUEL
FUEL
The Fuel Tank!
JEL
FUEL

The Fuel tank is like a car's tummy. You keep it full so that your car keeps on taking you places!

Don't forget to learn how to fill up that "tummy";

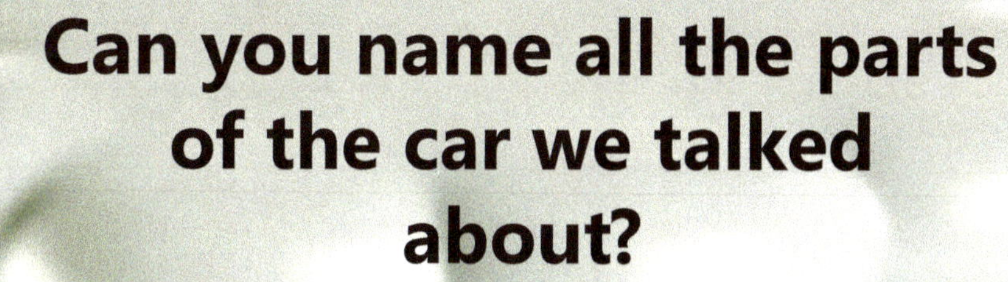
Can you name all the parts
of the car we talked
about?

FUN FACT:
Did you know that some cars can go faster than a cheetah!

VROOOOOM
FASTER THAN ME!

"Vroom Into Action" with Ali and Mr. Car as they take you on a fun ride! Learn what makes a car go vroom, roll, and stop. The perfect book for little car enthusiasts!"
MR. CAR